SURVIVING THE DARKNESS OF THE WAITING PERIOD

"Finding Strength in the Shadows: Strategies for Embracing the Darkness and Emerging Stronger"

BLESS P. WALTON

TABLE OF CONTENTS

CHAPTER 1

NAVIGATING THE ABYSS

In the journey of life, there are moments when we find ourselves in a seemingly endless waiting period, a space where time stretches its limits, and uncertainty looms like an ominous cloud. This chapter delves into the intricacies of this waiting period, aiming to shed light on the abyss that often accompanies it and providing insights on how to navigate through the darkness.

1.1 Understanding the Waiting Period

The waiting period is a paradoxical realm, a space where time seems to lose its usual cadence. It's a phase that can manifest in various aspects of life — waiting for a job offer, awaiting medical test results, or even anticipating a significant life change. Understanding this period requires a deep dive into its nuances.

The waiting period is not merely the absence of action; it is an active state of being. It demands a unique set of coping mechanisms as individuals grapple with the unknown. Often, the initial reaction to waiting is discomfort, restlessness, and a desire for resolution. However, comprehending the significance of this period allows individuals to reframe their perspective.

This chapter explores the psychological and emotional dimensions of waiting, acknowledging that it is more than the ticking of the clock. It's an opportunity for introspection, self-discovery, and preparation for the next chapter in one's life. By understanding the waiting period, individuals can transform it from an ordeal to a transformative journey.

1.2 Embracing the Unknown

The unknown is a formidable adversary. It triggers fear, anxiety, and a sense of vulnerability. However, it is also a realm of endless possibilities. Embracing the unknown during the waiting period is not about recklessness; it is about acknowledging the uncertainty while cultivating resilience and adaptability.

This section explores strategies to embrace the unknown, encouraging individuals to view uncertainty as a blank canvas rather than a void. It delves into the concept that the waiting period is a gestation period, a time for ideas to incubate and potentials to unfold. By reframing the unknown as a canvas for personal and professional growth, individuals can navigate the abyss with a sense of purpose and anticipation rather than dread.

Moreover, embracing the unknown involves relinquishing control to a certain extent. It requires an acceptance that some aspects of life are beyond immediate influence, and the only control one possesses is over their reactions and mindset. Through anecdotes, psychological insights, and practical exercises, this chapter guides readers toward a mindset that not only tolerates but celebrates the unknown.

1.3 The Emotional Landscape of Waiting

The emotional rollercoaster that accompanies the waiting period is both complex and profound. From hope and anticipation to fear and frustration, individuals experience a kaleidoscope of emotions during this time. Understanding this emotional landscape is crucial for navigating the abyss with resilience.

This section delves into the various emotions that may surface during the waiting period, providing a nuanced understanding of each. It acknowledges the legitimacy of emotions, emphasizing that feeling anxious or impatient does not equate to weakness. Instead, it recognizes these emotions as natural responses to the uncertainty that the waiting period brings.

Furthermore, this chapter introduces strategies for emotional regulation. From mindfulness techniques to expressive writing, individuals are guided to navigate the waves of emotions with grace and self-compassion. By fostering emotional intelligence, individuals can transform the waiting period from a source of distress to an opportunity for emotional growth.

In conclusion, Chapter 1 lays the foundation for the exploration of surviving the darkness of the waiting period. It prompts readers to understand the multifaceted nature of this phase, embrace the unknown with resilience, and navigate the emotional landscape with self-awareness. As individuals learn to tread these waters, they prepare themselves for the transformative journey that lies ahead.

CHAPTER 2
ILLUMINATING THE SHADOWS

In the midst of the waiting period, where uncertainty and darkness often prevail, the quest for light becomes paramount. Chapter 2, "Illuminating the Shadows," is a guide through the process of finding that light. It explores the art of resilience, strategies for emotional wellness, and the profound impact of embracing positivity even in the darkest of times.

2.1 Finding Light in the Darkness

The analogy of finding light in the darkness is powerful, evoking the image of a beacon guiding ships through tumultuous waters. In the waiting period, darkness can manifest in the form of doubt, anxiety, and a pervasive feeling of being stuck. This section explores how individuals can actively seek and create light, transforming the waiting period from a gloomy tunnel to a path illuminated with possibilities.

Finding light involves a shift in perspective. It encourages individuals to focus on what can be learned and gained during this period rather than dwelling on what is lacking. Through narratives of individuals who have successfully navigated their waiting periods, readers are inspired to see opportunities for growth, skill development, and personal enrichment.

Moreover, this section delves into the power of gratitude. In the midst of uncertainty, acknowledging and appreciating the positive aspects of life can act as a catalyst for change.

Practical exercises and reflective prompts guide readers to cultivate a mindset of gratitude, enabling them to find and amplify the light that exists even in the darkest corners of the waiting period.

2.2 Cultivating Resilience

Resilience is the backbone of surviving the darkness. It is the ability to bounce back from adversity and to endure challenges with strength and grace. This section explores the concept of resilience in the context of the waiting period, emphasizing that it is not just about enduring but about thriving despite the challenges.

Through psychological insights and real-world examples, readers are guided to understand the components of resilience —

adaptability, perseverance, and a growth mindset. The chapter encourages individuals to view setbacks as stepping stones rather than roadblocks, fostering a sense of agency and control even in the face of uncertainty.

Additionally, this section introduces practical strategies for cultivating resilience. Mindfulness practices, positive affirmations, and the development of a strong support system are explored as tools to bolster resilience. By weaving these practices into the fabric of daily life, individuals can build a resilient foundation that not only sustains them through the waiting period but also equips them for future challenges.

2.3 Strategies for Emotional Wellness

Emotional wellness is a cornerstone of navigating the shadows. The waiting period often stirs a cauldron of emotions, and managing these emotions effectively is crucial for maintaining overall well-being. This section delves into actionable strategies for emotional wellness, providing readers with a toolkit to navigate the emotional landscape with intention and self-awareness.

One of the key strategies explored is the practice of mindfulness. Care includes focusing on the current second without judgment. Through mindfulness exercises and meditations, individuals can cultivate a heightened awareness of their thoughts and emotions, promoting emotional regulation and resilience.

Expressive arts, such as journaling and creative outlets, are also highlighted as powerful tools for emotional wellness. These practices provide a safe space for individuals to process their emotions, gain clarity, and find a sense of catharsis. The chapter offers prompts and activities to encourage readers to explore these creative avenues as a means of promoting emotional well-being.

Furthermore, the importance of maintaining a healthy work-life balance is discussed. The waiting period can be all-consuming, and individuals may find solace in dedicating time to activities they enjoy. Whether it's a hobby, exercise, or spending time with loved ones, these activities contribute to emotional wellness by fostering a sense of fulfillment and connection.

In conclusion, Chapter 2 serves as a guide to illuminate the shadows of the waiting period. It encourages individuals to actively find light in the darkness, cultivate resilience as a foundational strength, and employ practical strategies for emotional wellness. By embracing positivity and building emotional strength, individuals not only endure the waiting period but emerge from it with a renewed sense of purpose and inner strength.

CHAPTER 3
THE ART OF PATIENCE

In a world that often demands immediate results and swift resolutions, the concept of patience can feel like an elusive virtue. Chapter 3, "The Art of Patience," invites readers to explore the profound impact of embracing patience during the waiting period. It unpacks the complexities of impatience, illuminates the transformative power of patience, and provides practical insights for developing a patient mindset.

3.1 Unpacking Impatience

Impatience is a common companion during the waiting period. It manifests as the restless tapping of fingers, the incessant checking of clocks, and the yearning for a quick resolution. This section delves into the roots of impatience, exploring it as a natural response to uncertainty and a desire for control.

Understanding impatience involves recognizing its detrimental effects on mental well-being. Impatience can breed frustration, anxiety, and a sense of helplessness. Through real-world examples and psychological insights, readers are guided to unpack their own impatience, identifying the triggers and acknowledging its impact on their emotional state.

Moreover, this section explores the cultural and societal factors that contribute to the glorification of speed and instant gratification. By unraveling the threads of societal expectations, readers gain a deeper understanding of why impatience has become a prevalent emotion and how it can be addressed at its core.

3.2 Transformative Power of Patience

Patience is not merely the absence of impatience; it is a proactive stance toward waiting. This section explores the transformative power of patience, framing it as a virtue that goes beyond endurance. Patience is portrayed as an active engagement with the present, a conscious choice to embrace the unfolding journey rather than fixating on the destination.

Through narratives of individuals who have harnessed the transformative power of patience, readers are inspired to see waiting as an opportunity for personal and spiritual growth. Patience, when cultivated intentionally, becomes a catalyst for resilience, gratitude, and a deepened understanding of oneself.

Furthermore, the chapter introduces the concept of "patient presence." This involves being fully engaged in the present moment, extracting meaning and value from the waiting period rather than viewing it as a mere pause in life. Practical exercises guide readers to develop the skill of patient presence, allowing them to savor the richness of each moment and find fulfillment in the journey itself.

3.3 Developing a Patient Mindset

Developing a patient mindset is a conscious and ongoing process. This section provides readers with actionable strategies to cultivate patience in their daily lives. It begins by reframing the perception of time, encouraging individuals to see waiting as a natural part of the human experience rather than an obstacle to be overcome.

The chapter explores the role of perspective in developing patience. By widening the lens through which individuals view their waiting period, they can gain a more holistic understanding of their circumstances. This involves acknowledging both the challenges and the opportunities that waiting presents.

Moreover, this section introduces the concept of "mindful waiting." Drawing from mindfulness practices, individuals are guided to approach the waiting period with a sense of curiosity and openness. Mindful waiting involves observing thoughts and emotions without judgment, allowing individuals to respond to their circumstances with greater clarity and composure.

The chapter concludes with the idea that developing a patient mindset is not a one-size-fits-all endeavor. It is a personalized journey that involves self-reflection, adaptability, and a commitment to continuous growth. By embracing the art of patience, individuals not only endure the waiting period more gracefully but also cultivate a mindset that serves them well in all aspects of life.

In summary, Chapter 3 delves into the art of patience as a transformative force during the waiting period. It unpacks the layers of impatience, illuminates the power of patience as an active choice, and provides practical strategies for developing a patient mindset.

Through this exploration, readers are invited to embrace waiting not as a hindrance but as a canvas for the cultivation of patience and personal growth.

CHAPTER 4

STRENGTH IN STILLNESS

In the whirlwind of the waiting period, where uncertainty dances and anxiety looms, finding strength in stillness becomes an invaluable skill. Chapter 4, "Strength in Stillness," delves into the transformative power of embracing quietude during moments of anticipation. It explores the harnessing of stillness, introduces mindfulness practices tailored for waiting, and delves into the profound inner strength that can be built through contemplation.

4.1 Harnessing the Power of Stillness

Stillness is not merely the absence of movement; it is a deliberate and potent state of being. This section explores the concept of harnessing the power of stillness during the waiting period. In a world that often glorifies constant activity, embracing moments of quiet contemplation becomes a revolutionary act.

Readers are guided to understand stillness as a source of strength, a sanctuary where the mind can find respite from the noise of uncertainty. Through anecdotes and philosophical insights, this section illuminates how moments of stillness can serve as anchors, providing individuals with a sense of stability amidst the tumultuous sea of waiting.

Moreover, this section introduces the idea of "active stillness." It is a practice that involves not only physical stillness but also cultivating a calm and focused mind amid external chaos. Practical exercises guide readers to incorporate active stillness into their daily lives, empowering them to navigate the waiting period with a centered and composed demeanor.

4.2 Mindfulness Practices for Waiting

Mindfulness, with its roots in ancient contemplative traditions, emerges as a guiding light in the darkness of the waiting period. This section explores tailored mindfulness practices designed to help individuals navigate the challenges of waiting. Mindfulness becomes a tool for cultivating awareness, managing stress, and fostering a deep connection with the present moment.

The chapter introduces breath awareness as a foundational mindfulness practice. Through guided exercises, readers learn to anchor their attention to the breath, creating a space of tranquility amidst the chaos. Mindful breathing becomes a companion during moments of impatience, providing individuals with a tangible and accessible way to center themselves.

Body scan meditation is another mindfulness practice explored in this section. It involves systematically bringing attention to different parts of the body, promoting relaxation and a heightened awareness of physical sensations. In the waiting period, where tension can build, the body scan becomes a valuable practice for releasing stress and fostering a sense of ease.

Additionally, the chapter delves into the concept of "mindful waiting." This involves applying mindfulness principles to the waiting experience itself. By observing thoughts and emotions without attachment, individuals can navigate the waiting period with a sense of equanimity, free from the rollercoaster of anticipation and anxiety.

4.3 Building Inner Strength through Contemplation

Contemplation becomes a bridge to inner strength during the waiting period. This section explores the art of introspection and thoughtful reflection as a means of building resilience and clarity. Contemplation is not a passive activity; it is an active engagement with one's thoughts and emotions.

Readers are guided through contemplative practices that encourage self-inquiry. Journaling becomes a powerful tool for capturing thoughts, emotions, and insights during the waiting period. By putting pen to paper, individuals externalize their internal experiences, gaining clarity and perspective on their journey.

Furthermore, the chapter explores the practice of gratitude contemplation. In the midst of uncertainty, deliberately reflecting on what one is grateful for becomes a transformative act. This practice shifts the focus from what is lacking to what is present, fostering a mindset of abundance and resilience.

Moreover, this section delves into the practice of future envisioning. Contemplating a positive future, despite the uncertainties of the present, becomes a source of motivation and inspiration. Through guided exercises, individuals are encouraged to envision the outcomes they desire, instilling a sense of purpose and direction during the waiting period.

In conclusion, Chapter 4 unfolds the concept of finding strength in stillness during the waiting period. It explores the deliberate harnessing of stillness, introduces mindfulness practices tailored for waiting, and delves into the transformative power of contemplation. By embracing these practices, individuals not only endure the waiting period but also emerge from it with a newfound inner strength and resilience.

Embrace the wisdom within these pages, discover the strength that lies in stillness, and emerge from the shadows of waiting as a person fortified by the lessons learned. Your journey to finding strength in the darkness starts here. Are you ready to embark on the path to emerging stronger?

A Book By DivineFavour Onofuevure
DELIVERY WITHOUT STRESS
A Higher Chance Of Safely Delivering A Healthy Child